Future-Proofing Students
Entrepreneurship Skills in the Classroom

Table of Contents

Chapter 1. Introduction

Special Report: Future-Proofing Students: Entrepreneurship Skills in the Classroom

In this exceptional Special Report, we dive headfirst into the rapidly changing landscape of education and career readiness. 'Future-Proofing Students: Entrepreneurship Skills in the Classroom' is a thrilling exploration of how revolutionary educational frameworks that introduce entrepreneurial skills can better equip our students with the ability to thrive in the future. Driven by fascinating insights, vibrant case studies, and cutting-edge strategies from industry leaders globally, this report showcases the importance of fostering an entrepreneurial spirit at a young age. Ignite your curiosity and join us on this engrossing journey, as we unveil the transformative equation of education and entrepreneurship. Reading this report isn't just an action; it's an investment in a future where our students are not just job seekers but job creators! Be captivated, be enlightened, and most importantly, be inspired to participate in this incredible shift in academic paradigms. Don't miss the opportunity to arm yourself with this wealth of knowledge – the positive ripple effect can be tremendous!

Chapter 2. The Dawn of Educational Evolution: Need for Entrepreneurship Skills

Given the ever-evolving conditions of the modern world, the stakes for education have never been higher. It is increasingly crucial for educators to not only impart knowledge but instill practical skills that will equip students for an unpredictable future. Amid this shift, one key skill-set stands out: entrepreneurship.

While the term "entrepreneurship" might conjure images of high-flying tech pioneer or a local business owner taking bold leaps in business development, it also encapsulates a baseline mindset and skill-set necessary for navigating and leading in the future of work and society.

2.1. Defining Entrepreneurship Skills

Entrepreneurship skills can be broadly categorized into three main areas:

1. Creative Problem-Solving: Being able to identify challenges, opportunities, and solutions in unique, imaginative ways.

2. Risk-taking: Fearlessly taking calculated risks and learning from both success and failure alike.

3. Future-Oriented Thinking: Thinking big, long-term and strategically about the future.

These skills not just increase employment prospects but also promote resourcefulness, resilience, and adaptability. They equip young minds to handle any uncertain situations or unanticipated problems, encouraging them to think outside the box creatively and innovatively.

2.2. Understanding the Shift in Education Landscape

The advent of disruptive technologies, coupled with the rapid changes in the global economy, has necessitated a need for a dynamic and adaptable workforce. The traditional model of education, structured around rote learning and siloed disciplines, is inadequate for facing these novel challenges.

Education systems require a paradigm shift that allows students to contextualize academic learnings within the framework of real-world scenarios. Integrating entrepreneurial skills in educational curriculums places emphasis on innovative thinking, critical analysis, and practical problem-solving. It encourages the development of a growth mindset, enabling students to embrace challenges, persevere against setbacks, and view effort as a natural path to mastery.

2.3. Case Study: Finland's Innovative Approach to Education

Consider the case of Finland, which has notably introduced phenomena-based learning into its educational system. Students examine 'phenomena,' complex real-world issues, from different viewpoints; for example, global warming can be studied from the angles of geography, economics, and even ethics. This kind of learning fosters a highly adaptive and cross-disciplinary mindset, deeply ingraining entrepreneurial thinking into its students.

2.4. Contemporary Teaching Strategies for Fostering Entrepreneurship

Incorporating entrepreneurial skills in the classroom does not require blowing up the current curriculum. Instead, it involves introducing innovative teaching strategies in line with the entrepreneurial mindset. Here are some strategies:

1. Project-Based Learning: This reflects the working style of the future, where creative problem-solving and collaboration are core requirements.

2. Learning by Doing: This method encourages active learning, helping students to better understand how their academic knowledge can be utilized practically in the real world.

3. Interdisciplinary Teaching: This aims to break the silos of subject disciplines and encourage multifaceted thinking, making students agile and adaptive to different scenarios.

These contemporary teaching strategies play a critical role in nurturing the requisite skill-set for students to flourish in an ever-evolving professional landscape.

2.5. The Role of Technology

Technology will continue to be an intrinsic part of this disruptive educational shift. Its role primarily includes simplified content delivery, remote and flexible learning opportunities, and provision of vast information directly accessible to students. For instance, virtual reality can simulate business scenarios, helping students learn to recognize opportunities and make strategic decisions.

2.6. Conclusion: A Transformed Education

The introduction of entrepreneurship skills in the classroom is not just a testament to the evolving educational landscape but also a proactive response to the rapidly transforming global economy. By fostering an entrepreneurial spirit, we expand our students' horizons to think bigger, think different. They become creators, innovators, and leaders, rather than just receivers of information or job applicants. In essence, the future-proofing of students lies in embracing this dawn of educational evolution.

Future generations will inhabit a world we can't fully predict, solve problems we may not yet perceive, and create opportunities we can't even imagine. Our best approach to preparing these young minds lies in teaching them to understand, navigate, and most importantly, shape this unpredictable landscape. That is the entrepreneurial spirit, and that is why we must prioritize the development of these entrepreneurship skills in our learning environments. The dawn of educational evolution is here, and the need for entrepreneurial skills couldn't be more essential.

It's about fostering the integral skills that navigate the meanders of life, not just career. The call for entrepreneurial skills is not a call to produce more entrepreneurs, but to nurture individuals prepared for the complexities and opportunities of an uncertain and exciting future. After all, the most entrepreneurial thing we can teach our youth is the belief in their ability to innovate, create, and shape their world.

Chapter 3. Redefining Learning: Integrating Entrepreneurship in Curriculum

In recent times, we have seen a compelling deviation from traditional pedagogical methods. Modern educators are ever more inclined towards imparting practical skills rather than purely rote-based learning. There's an increasing recognition that entrepreneurial skills, like creativity, resilience, and the ability to identify opportunities, need to be instilled from an early age. Integrating entrepreneurship into curriculum can create an integral shift from a superficial understanding of theoretical aspects to acquiring profound, practical knowledge.

3.1. A Paradigm Shift in Education

The concept of education has evolved dramatically over the past few decades. Traditional rote learning methods have ceded ground to an approach that values self-exploration, critical thinking, and proactivity on the part of the students. Learners are now encouraged to take ownership of their education, questioning, exploring, and building knowledge through their inquiry.

Inspired by the startup culture and acknowledging the linear connection between entrepreneurship and these 21st century skills, educationists globally are rallying behind the integration of entrepreneurship in the curriculum. Rooting it into the learning culture ignites a shift from knowledge consumers to knowledge creators.

3.2. Pioneering Entrepreneurial Learning

At the heart of entrepreneurial education lies the challenge to instill core entrepreneurship skills such as problem-solving, creative thinking, resilience, team-working, and opportunity identification. This necessitates a blend of theory and practice, wherein students can explore and experiment freely without the fear of failure. Classroom discussions, guest lectures from successful entrepreneurs, and hands-on experience with startup challenges can provide students with invaluable experiential learning.

Entrepreneurship-themed competitions and business simulations infuse a sense of excitement and immersion, making education an enjoyable journey rather than a burdensome chore. Meanwhile, mentoring programs and internships provide the practical exposure and guidance that students require.

3.3. Curriculum Development

While implementing entrepreneurial education, it's crucial that it is seamlessly integrated into the existing curriculum rather than treated as an add-on. Curriculum developers must focus on immersive learning experiences that build entrepreneurial competencies on top of the existing knowledge base.

An ideal entrepreneurial curriculum would identify key concepts that overlap with traditional subjects. For instance, the mathematical principle of compound interest could be taught in the context of finance and investment. Simultaneously, students could be engaged in dual-purpose projects – ones that address their curriculum while fostering skills like team collaboration, leadership, and problem-solving.

3.4. Teacher Training: A Pillar of Success

Any drastic change in curriculum demands an equally intensive shift in the teacher training paradigm. Teachers themselves need to adopt an entrepreneurial mindset to effectively guide students on their entrepreneurial journeys. They must be comfortable with fostering independence and creativity, allowing students to fail and learn from their mistakes, and being facilitators rather than mere information providers.

A transformation of this magnitude requires comprehensive teacher training programs that breed familiarity with entrepreneurship, its principles, and the diverse teaching methods required.

3.5. The Impact: Gearing for a Brighter Future

Evidence from early adopters of entrepreneurial education shows a multitude of benefits. Beyond just cultivating a new generation of entrepreneurs, we're fostering a generation of problem solvers, leaders, and innovators, capable of adapting to the continually evolving future.

The introduction of entrepreneurial learning enhances critical thinking, problem-solving skills, financial literacy, resilience, and empathy among students. This holistic approach not only prepares them for their future careers but also enables them to contribute positively to their communities.

All things considered, the incorporation of entrepreneurship in the curriculum seems less like an option and more like a necessary revolution. As education becomes more forward-looking and tailored to the evolving dynamics of the future, integrating entrepreneurship seems both a logical and compelling step forward. It requires a comprehensive approach encompassing curriculum changes, teacher transformation, and amendments in the ways we assess and evaluate learning. The resultant equation promises not only to nurture students ready for the future but also to establish a global society that thrives on innovation and mutual growth.

Chapter 4. From Theory to Practice: Hands-On Entrepreneurship Education

The transformational journey from theoretical learning to practical application is fascinating. And, when it comes to entrepreneurship education, this process is crucial to pave the way for students to become real-world problem solvers.

As we delve into this exciting world, we will witness innovative pedagogical strategies, practical examples, and captivating insights into how educators are facilitating students' transition from passive learners to proactive doers.

4.1. The Paradigm Shift From Conventional Classrooms

The conventional classroom's normative instructional methods often limit students' ability to apply their learnings in an entrepreneurial context. In contrast, hands-on entrepreneurship education facilitates an experiential learning approach, ensuring that students attain the essential skills to thrive as future entrepreneurs.

Enabling students to apply theoretical concepts practically provides them an opportunity to learn and adapt to the varied entrepreneurial situations that they will face in their future careers. The hands-on approach promotes critical thinking, decision-making, and problem-solving skills - all of these are core constituents of an entrepreneurial mindset.

4.2. Adaptive Learning Through Role-Play

A remarkable pedagogical method adopted in hands-on entrepreneurship education is role-play simulations. These activities are designed to mimic real-world entrepreneurial scenarios. The participative nature of role playing helps students to gain insights into the complexities of an entrepreneurial journey and comprehend how decisions impact business outcomes.

Role-playing scenarios range from analyzing case studies to executing a pitch for investors. It promotes collaboration, negotiation skills, and the ability to cope with failure – fostering resilience and perseverance, the critical attributes of a successful entrepreneur.

4.3. Entrepreneurship Boot Camps: Catalysts of Change

Entrepreneurship boot camps are intensive training programs that expose students to the practical facets of starting and running a business. These boot camps typically encompass activities like ideation sessions, business model canvassing, and pitching to real or simulated investors.

Boot camps provide a reality check, while at the same time imbuing students with the necessary determination, tenacity, and leadership qualities. They also foster a competitive environment that simulates the real-world nature of entrepreneurship.

4.4. The Project-Based Learning Approach

Project-based learning (PBL) is a progressive teaching method whereby students learn by actively engaging in real-world projects. In the realm of entrepreneurship education, PBL encourages students to develop business ideas, conduct market feasibility studies, and even go as far as launching a start-up.

PBL promotes cross-curricular learning and encourages students to apply knowledge from different disciplines to solve complex problems. This holistic learning method equips would-be entrepreneurs with a wealth of practical experience and knowledge, making them better prepared for the volatile business terrain that awaits.

4.5. The Integration of Digital Technology in Entrepreneurship Education

Digital technology has further revolutionized the way entrepreneurship is taught in the classroom. Online collaboration tools, virtual business simulations, e-commerce platforms, and social media marketing are just a few examples of how digital technology is being leveraged in practical entrepreneurship education.

The integration of digital technology in hands-on entrepreneurship education not only enhances learning but also equips students with the tech-savviness required in today's digitally dominated business world.

4.6. The Crucial Role of Mentoring in Entrepreneurship Education

The role of mentors in hands-on entrepreneurship education cannot be overstated. Mentorship offers an invaluable opportunity for students to learn from experienced entrepreneurs. The insights gleaned from these direct interactions provide a realistic perspective on entrepreneurship, beyond the confines of a classroom.

The bridge between theory and practice lies in kindling an entrepreneurial spirit within students and providing them with ample opportunities to experiment, learn, and grow. By implementing hands-on strategies in entrepreneurship education, educators can instil an entrepreneurial mindset in their students, equipping them to successfully navigate the unpredictability of the future entrepreneurial landscape.

Chapter 5. Case Studies: Successful Implementations Around the Globe

Schools across the world have gained momentum in the revitalization of their curriculum, incorporating entrepreneurial skills into their approach. This shift is responsible for creating innovative and resilient youngsters ready to engage in an ever-evolving global market. We'll dive into five globetrotting case studies, from highly diverse backgrounds, that are crafting a future generation of entrepreneurs.

5.1. Finland: Launchpad to Innovation

Finland has exemplified its commitment to inculcating an innovative spirit in its students by establishing Me & MyCity. It's an award-winning education innovation that provides 12-year-olds with an understanding of entrepreneurship, the economy, and society. Inside the Me & MyCity learning environment, the students work in a profession, earn a salary, and function as consumers and citizens.

In just 2019, Me & MyCity had an impressive reach, involving a total of 75,000 Finnish schoolchildren. The unique pedagogical method focuses on proficiency, transversal skills, and multidisciplinary project-based learning, marking a significant move towards entrepreneurship education.

5.2. USA: Inspiring Entrepreneurial Mindsets in the Heartland

Jaime Casap, former Google Education Evangelist, famously said: "Don't ask a student what she wants to be when she grows up. Ask her what problem she wants to solve." This idea is the cornerstone of the entrepreneurship education at the Beloit Junior/Senior High School, Kansas. Students engage in real-world problem-solving, a critical component of entrepreneurial education, through launching micro-businesses and learning the consequences of their decisions.

Beloit's focus on entrepreneurship education isn't singular. The Network For Teaching Entrepreneurship (NFTE) has made it its mission to equip under-resourced students from various parts of the U.S. with entrepreneurial skills, signaling a larger shift towards entrepreneurial pedagogic frameworks.

5.3. Australia: An Integrated Approach

Australia doesn't fall far behind in this race. The Australian Government launched the Australian Blueprint for Career Development, which succinctly integrates entrepreneurial skills. The Alice Springs School of the Air, for example, empowers its students with the necessary entrepreneurial skills through programs like Mini-economy. Students undertake roles such as managing an economy, making key policy decisions, and dealing with socio-economic issues. They learn essential entrepreneurial skills like taking initiative, financial management, and decision making.

5.4. Norway: Fostering Innovators at a Young Age

The Norwegian primary school, Ringstabekk, stands out in its approach to teach an entrepreneurship-focused curriculum. Every student from ages 6-16 contributes to their Young Enterprise scheme, with older students acting as CEOs and CFOs of "student companies," while younger ones function as employees. This hands-on approach nurtures entrepreneurial attitudes like risk-taking, innovativeness, cooperation, and understanding of business functions.

5.5. India: Redefining Education Framework

In India, too, tides are shifting. The National Entrepreneurship Network (NEN) has implemented entrepreneurship programs in over 500 colleges. They provide training, mentorship and support to students, an effort that has led to the creation of 2,000+ new start-ups over the past decade.

Significantly, the Atal Tinkering Labs, driven by Atal Innovation Mission, NITI Aayog, provides play-work spaces where students can understand the concepts of innovation and entrepreneurship. Their work aims to shape inventors of the future by fostering curiosity, creativity, and imagination amongst young minds.

The transversal, global adoption of entrepreneurship education stands testament to its criticality. A multidimensional future awaits students as they learn to navigate real-world challenges, make informed decisions, and become proactive contributors to society. As sown from these case studies, the seeds of entrepreneurial skills are being sown at school level, and we can confidently anticipate a future where students aren't just job seekers but job creators.

Chapter 6. Skills for Tomorrow: Essential Entrepreneurial Skills for Students

The contemporary instructional framework should move beyond its conventional confines to encompass Entrepreneurship Education (EE). The skill set taught through EE can imbue students with the wherewithal to navigate the uncertain job landscape of the future.

6.1. The Need for Entrepreneurial Skills

Traditional education has revolved around building knowledge, both theoretical and applied. However, with rapid shifts in the employment landscape, the need for innovation, creativity, and adaptability, among other skills, is increasingly coming to the fore. As automation pervades workplaces and typical job nature changes, there's a need to inculcate entrepreneurial skills in students, arming them for tomorrow.

These skills, often referred to as 'the Entrepreneurial Skill Set', include creativity, critical thinking, problem-solving, resilience, and emotional intelligence. These skills foster an entrepreneurial mindset, equipping students with the ability to adapt and flourish in a continuously changing world.

6.2. Developing an Entrepreneurship Mindset: Essential Skills

An entrepreneurial mindset braces students for the realities of the fast-paced, ever-evolving future job market. This section dives into several critical entrepreneurial skills for students.

1. Innovation & Creativity: At the heart of entrepreneurship is creativity and innovation. These skills equip students with the ability to generate unique ideas, think outside the box, and foster innovation. For instance, introducing open-ended problems or design tasks can spur creativity in students.

2. Critical Thinking: Entrepreneurs must be able to assess situations and make informed decisions critically. This involves understanding problems, analyzing information, evaluating solutions, and reflecting on the outcome. Critical thinking skills can be fostered in the classroom through discussion-based lessons, problem-solving tasks, and debate sessions.

3. Resilience & Adaptability: The world of entrepreneurship is fraught with uncertainty and frequent changes. As such, a crucial skill for students is the ability to be resilient and adaptable in the face of challenges. These skills can be advocated in a learning environment that promotes risk-taking and embraces failure as part of the learning process.

4. Emotional Intelligence: EI refers to the ability to understand and manage one's emotions and those of others. For entrepreneurs, EI is vital for interpersonal communication, team management, and decision-making. Schools can inculcate EI through personal-social development programs and collaborative learning tasks.

6.3. Implementing Entrepreneurial Skill Development in Education

While there's a consensus that entrepreneurial skills are necessary, schools may struggle with the implementation aspect. It's not merely about teaching but about innovating the teaching methods. Here are some pointers for educators:

1. Cross-disciplinary learning: Entrepreneurship is not bounded by a single discipline or subject. It encompasses a wide range of areas. Hence, schools should encourage cross-disciplinary learning where entrepreneurial skills are intertwined within the existing curriculum.

2. Active learning: Schools must transition from passive to active learning. Encourage an atmosphere where students engage in brainstorming sessions, group projects, problem-solving tasks, and business simulations to simulate the entrepreneurial environment.

3. Interaction with Entrepreneurs: Regular interactions with entrepreneurs can provide students with practical understanding and inspiration. These sessions can take the form of guest lectures, workshops, or mentoring sessions.

4. Entrepreneurial projects and competitions: Encouraging students to take on entrepreneurial projects or participate in competitions can build real-life entrepreneurial skills, foster a sense of independence, and spur creative critical thinking.

6.4. Conclusion: The Future is Now

There is a growing urgency to empower students with entrepreneurial skills that will enable them to navigate the future job landscape effectively. The significance of these skills extends past traditional business applications to any innovative and creative endeavor in an increasingly volatile, uncertain, complex, and ambiguous world.

By evolving the education system to champion these skills, we can arm our students to not just secure jobs but create them. With the dawn of this new educational paradigm, we indeed step closer to future-proofing our students. As we end this chapter, let us not be complacent but be spurred into action. After all, the future is now.

The journey towards ingraining entrepreneurial skills in education may seem daunting but remember that every big journey begins with a small step. Let's take that step today for a better tomorrow. As Arthur Ashe famously said, "Start where you are. Use what you have. Do what you can."

Chapter 7. Big Picture Impact: How Entrepreneurship Education Influences Career Paths

While entrepreneurship education is often associated merely with creating a new venture, its wide-ranging impact extends much further. This education paradigm equips learners with a myriad of skills, becoming a driving force that alters their career pathways considerably. The competencies acquired through entrepreneurship education have proven to be instrumental in enabling students to navigate the complexities of present and future job markets effectively.

7.1. The Entrepreneurial Mindset

Entrepreneurship education cultivates an entrepreneurial mindset – a critical skillset that shapes the way individuals approach career opportunities. This mindset is typically characterized by principles of creativity, innovation, resilience, strategic thinking, being opportunity-oriented, and a willingness to take calculated risks. Even outside the boundaries of setting up new ventures, these ideals hold immense value.

For students, an entrepreneurial approach equips them to recognize and seize opportunities. They learn how to turn obstacles into business opportunities, displaying resilience while facing adversity. This not only empowers them to be self-starters but also aids in developing a zest for lifelong learning. As this mindset pervades their career decisions, they are more likely to pursue dynamic career paths and explore unconventional roles.

7.2. Transformative Life Skills

Entrepreneurship education brings about the development of a variety of practically applicable soft skills. These skills include communication, emotional intelligence, negotiation, networking, financial literacy, problem-solving, and decision-making, to name a few. Such abilities prove to be powerful assets in the job market, regardless of one's chosen career path.

These integral life skills form the backbone of professional personas. For instance, communication and negotiation skills allow individuals to articulate their ideas convincingly and negotiate better terms during business dealings. Networking skills facilitate the making of fruitful professional relationships, while financial literacy helps manage personal and organizational finances effectively.

Practical experiences of setting up and running a venture offer experiential learning opportunities. They help to reinforce concepts of time management, priority-setting, and strategic thinking. This environment encourages students to learn from their mistakes and iteratively improve their processes, extensively preparing them for their future careers.

7.3. Career adaptability: Navigating an Evolving Job Market

In an ever-evolving job market, the need for career adaptability has never been more pronounced. The advent of new technologies and shifting industry paradigms often lead to the emergence of novel professional roles while making others obsolete. This continuous career landscape transformation demands adaptability and versatility, hallmarks of an entrepreneurial mindset.

With an entrepreneurial education, students acquire abilities enabling them to remain agile and resilient, even when faced with unprecedented circumstances. Fearlessness in the face of failure, resourcefulness, and innovation allow them to pivot and adapt to the changing demands of the job market. Recognizing the untapped potential in emerging industries can lead to fulfilling and successful career endeavours.

The flexibility inherent in entrepreneurship education also prepares students for portfolio careers, where they juggle multiple roles across various sectors. Portfolio careers, a growing trend, can lead to diversified income sources, more significant learning opportunities, broader networks, and an enhanced ability to manage career risks.

7.4. Career Development and Job Creation

The ultimate impact of entrepreneurship education is evident in career development and job creation. Students who understand the dynamics of entrepreneurship are more likely to start successful enterprises. By fostering new businesses, they not only carve a niche for themselves but also create jobs, contributing positively to economic growth and social development.

Moreover, the entrepreneurial skills acquired through this educational paradigm encourage students to be career creators rather than job seekers. With innovation-focused thinking, these young entrepreneurs win the battle against unemployment by establishing job opportunities not just for themselves, but for others as well.

To conclude, the impact of entrepreneurship education on career pathways is profound and multifaceted. It cultivates an entrepreneurial mindset, develops key life skills, enhances career adaptability, and fosters job creation. Entrepreneurship education essentially future-proofs students, ensuring that they are not just ready to participate in the job market, but are equipped to lead and redefine it. Thus, incorporating entrepreneurship education into mainstream curriculums can create an enriching learning environment for students and prepare them for an ever-evolving world of work.

Chapter 8. Trailblazers: Schools Pioneering Innovative Approaches

Unquestionably, the game-changing move in the contemporary educational landscape is the integration of entrepreneurship skills into the classroom. There has been a seismic shift from supplying antiquated, rote-taught knowledge to building our students' capacity as potential trailblazers. With this new age dawned, schools across the globe are pioneering innovative approaches, incorporating elements of entrepreneurship. Below are some remarkable examples of these bold moves.

8.1. From Pupils to Founders: The Incorporation of Startup Culture

This initiative can be traced back to the "Young Entrepreneurs Academy" (YEA!). YEA! started in 2004 as an innovative educational program held at the University of Rochester. Over the years, the program has expanded across the United States, partnering with various institutions to train aspiring young entrepreneurs. The course, which runs from October through to May, covers all the facets of launching a startup, including idea generation, pitching, fundraising, creating business plans, and more. The YEA! franchise has inspired a wave of schools across America, grounding the essence of startup culture in their students from a young age.

8.2. Rethinking Traditional Fields: Entrepreneurial Science and Mathematics

A major shift is also on the horizon in traditional fields like science and mathematics. Due to innovative schools such as the Denver School of Innovation and Sustainable Design, these once heavily fact-based subjects have been revived with an entrepreneurial twist. They have deployed an integrated curriculum, where science and math classes merge with business strategies. This equips students with problem-solving and critical-thinking skills - skills that are vital cornerstones of successful entrepreneurship.

For instance, in a physics class, instead of the usual practice of solving textbook problems, students are met with real-world issues that require them to apply mathematical theorems and scientific laws toward viable solutions. These students aren't just solving Newton's Cradle; they're contemplating how to turn gravity into an efficient and green power source.

8.3. Cross-Cultural Entrepreneurial Collaboration

In Asia, the "Entrepreneurship High School" chain in South Korea boasts an unparalleled approach. They foster international collaborations enabling their students to experience entrepreneurship at a global scale. Partnering with counterparts in a range of countries, they engage their students in real-time virtual business simulations. The students then navigate the complications inherent to international trade, strategy, and communication. This noble attempt at creating a globalized experience from within the classroom walls is a testament to their innovation.

8.4. The Transition: From Classrooms to Business Incubators

Stepping into Europe, we find Finland's Espoo International School, which has taken a bold step by transitioning from traditional classrooms to business incubators. Giving their students access to a well-resourced hub for early-stage businesses, the school has created a platform where students can transform their ideas into startups under the guidance of experienced entrepreneurs. This challenging atmosphere fosters both the practical and theoretical knowledge needed to build a successful business.

8.5. Inclusive Entrepreneurship: Addressing Under-represented Groups

Venturing to South America, the 'Teach for Argentina' initiative deserves appreciation for their substantial efforts towards inclusive entrepreneurship. Recognizing the potential in lower socioeconomic strata, they have strived to equip disadvantaged students with entrepreneurial skills. Despite limited resources, these schools have incorporated business studies into their ordinary curriculum, exposing their students to entrepreneurial thinking early on.

Each of these schools have approached the integration of entrepreneurship into conventional education differently. But what binds them together is their common aim to equip our future generation with the skills they need to not just navigate, but also to shape the world. Their approaches may vary - be it through transforming traditional subjects, encouraging cross-cultural collaboration, creating a startup culture from scratch, or ensuring inclusivity - but their ultimate goal remains the same: to foster the entrepreneurial spirit in our students and empower them to become galvanized architects in our rapidly evolving world.

Chapter 9. Lessons from the Frontlines: Educators' Perspectives on Teaching Entrepreneurship

Educators worldwide are increasingly recognizing the power and necessity of incorporating entrepreneurship education in their curriculums. The process of teaching entrepreneurship isn't simply about imparting business skills; it is about molding a can-do, innovative, and resilient mentality in students. In this deep-diving chapter, we explore the perspective of educators on teaching entrepreneurship, drawing from their experiences and proven strategies that have found success in diverse classroom surroundings.

9.1. Lessons from Different Geographies

Education, culture, and socio-economic conditions greatly influence the manner in which entrepreneurship is taught and perceived. A teacher in Silicon Valley may emphasize tech entrepreneurship, whereas an educator in rural Ghana might focus on agriculture-based enterprises. Classroom experiences differ vastly across continents, and through these diverse stories, one can learn unique approaches to teaching entrepreneurship.

```
|===
| Location | Key Entrepreneurial Lessons

| Silicon Valley, USA | Technology-focused. Encourage
```

risk-taking and learning from failure.
| Rural Gnana | Agricultural entrepreneurship. Uphold sustainable and locally beneficial practices.
| Industrial China | Production and efficiency. Harness the power of technological advancements.
| Student-centered Finland | Lifelong learning practices. Foster innovativeness and initiative.
|===

These examples illustrate the need to adapt the curriculum based on local industries and cultures, integrating the entrepreneurial journey with practical, locally relevant experiences.

=== Balancing Theory and Practice

A consistent theme across all educators' perspectives is the need to balance theory and practice. While theoretical knowledge provides a solid foundation, it does not suffice on its own in a real-world setting that values execution over ideas.

Educators have repeatedly emphasized the role of applied learning activities, such as starting viable mini-businesses within the school setting. Such exercises bring about an experience of the real-world rewards, disappointments, and unpredictability involved in enterprise creation.

=== Personal Development and Entrepreneurship

A critical yet often overlooked aspect of teaching entrepreneurship is its relation to personal development. Emotional intelligence, problem-solving, self-motivation—these traits reside at the heart of a successful entrepreneur. Teachers have found immense benefits in weaving personal development into entrepreneurship education.

An instructor may facilitate this by emphasizing goal-setting, resilience training, or team-building exercises. Such a holistic approach fosters not just business-oriented thinkers but individuals better equipped to handle life's challenges.

Enabling Creativity and Innovation

In an era defined by rapid technological advancement, creativity and innovation are invaluable assets. To instill this mindset, many educators are departing from traditional teaching methods, instead employing strategies that break convention and encourage original thinking.

Educational tools that accommodate brainstorming, prototyping, and feedback loops have become key to training students to think outside the box and dare to disrupt. These enabling environments foster creativity that could translate into groundbreaking entrepreneurial ideas.

Engaging Parents and Communities

The teaching of entrepreneurship transcends the boundaries of the classroom. Active parent and community participation can strengthen the effectiveness of these programs. Educators have learned that parents and community members can serve as role models and offer real-life case studies, contributing immensely to the learning process.

To conclude, teaching entrepreneurship, as told by educators, is a dynamic, multifaceted process. It requires a balanced and context-sensitive approach, incorporating local culture, personal development, innovative teaching methods, and community involvement. Most critically, it's about creating an environment that ignites passion, fosters resilience, promotes creativity, and empowers students to take a leap of faith.

Road Forward: Policy Changes to Support Entrepreneurship Education

The concept of education has changed drastically in the past couple of decades, especially in the light of steadily accelerating technological innovation and globalization. As we stand at the threshold of a new wave of digital revolution, national and international policies need to be adapted in a way that can cater to this shift. Implementing entrepreneurial education effectively calls for systemic changes from the ground up. Below we delve into possible ways forward regarding policy changes.

Fostering an Entrepreneurship-focused Curriculum

An essential step is to reimagine the current curriculums provided at schools. Traditional models of pedagogy often fail to keep up with the rapidly changing career landscape. Consequently, educational systems might consider adopting a more entrepreneurship-centered curriculum. Such a curriculum should encompass core entrepreneurial competences, such as autonomy, adaptability, creativity, initiative, problem-solving, and team building.

Understanding and implementing these changes can also be

facilitated by developing teacher guidelines and training models. Offering teachers the opportunity to familiarize themselves with the entrepreneurial approach is crucial. Suitable material and training would guarantee that not only can educators understand the value of these skills, but they are able to effectively instill them into the classroom environment.

Prioritizing Entrepreneurial Education at All Levels

There is often a misconception that entrepreneurship skills should only be taught at the university level. However, laying the groundwork for entrepreneurial thinking should begin as early as possible. Early exposure to entrepreneurial concepts can promote a shift from rote learning to problem-solving and creativity-fueled curriculum from elementary levels. This should be mirrored in policy changes that prioritize the inclusion of entrepreneurial education across all grades.

The policy changes needed are not only limited to elementary, middle, and high schools but should also extend to higher education. Courses on entrepreneurship should be on offer across faculties, breaking the boundaries typically confining entrepreneurship to business studies. Stipulating entrepreneurship as a cross-disciplinary subject can help foster a university-wide culture of entrepreneurship.

Partnerships and Stakeholder Engagement

Achieving substantial changes in the educational landscape requires concerted efforts of various stakeholders ranging from educators, school administrators, the business sector, and government. Policies must promote partnerships between schools and the local business communities to provide students with practical experiences such as internships, mentorship programs, or startup competitions. These school-community partnerships can create a rich environment for budding entrepreneurs.

Government policies should also encourage non-governmental organizations and corporate sectors to participate in entrepreneurship education. This could be achieved by offering monetary incentives like tax breaks or by acknowledging their contributions to society.

Infrastructure for Entrepreneurial Learning

Infrastructure plays an indispensable role in promoting entrepreneurial learning. While it is essential to introduce changes to the curriculum and teacher training, it is equally important to modify the physical infrastructure of learning institutions to support entrepreneurship.

Active learning classrooms equipped with innovative educational technologies can significantly promote entrepreneurial learning. These changes could include the development of on-site innovation hubs, technology-rich classrooms and dedicated spaces for brainstorming sessions or entrepreneurial projects.

Government policies can play a double role here. First, by setting mandatory guidelines for academic institutions to dedicate a certain part of their infrastructure to promote entrepreneurial learning. Second, by providing funds or grants to assist schools with this transformation.

Standardized Evaluation and Success Metrics

The effects of any policy changes can only be viewed through a lens of standardized evaluation and success metrics. A shift towards entrepreneurship education may necessitate changes to the standardized evaluations. Instead of heavily relying on testing academic knowledge, the policies should promote the use of rubrics to assess entrepreneurial skills, attitudes, and behaviors.

In conclusion, the path forward requires consistent engagement from several stakeholders including educators, students, government and non-governmental organizations, communities, and businesses. A paradigm shift of this magnitude may involve challenges, but the rewards are unarguably transformative, both for the students and society at large. With the right policies promoting entrepreneurial education, we can help mould the job creators of the future, and in the process, contribute to a resilient global economy.

Looking Ahead: Predicting The Future of Entrepreneurship Education

As we gaze into the future of entrepreneurship education, it is essential to unravel the tectonic shifts in pedagogical themes, evolving students' needs, industrial trends, and their collective impact. A panorama unfolds before us that is intricate but plausible, complex yet fascinating.

The Role of Emerging Technologies

Education, in its traditional sense, has been a rigid structure. However, with the advent of emerging technologies such as Artificial Intelligence (AI), Machine Learning (ML), Augmented Reality (AR), Virtual

Reality (VR), and Internet of Things (IoT), a metamorphosis is underway.

In the sphere of entrepreneurship education, these technologies hold colossal potential. Imagine a classroom where students can brainstorm startup ideas in an AR-enabled creative ambience, or a curriculum that banks on AI to facilitate personalized learning paths. The prospective contribution of ML in analyzing learners' style and customizing course materials also deserves mention. Therefore, while predicting the future of entrepreneurship education, it is impossible to omit the role of these groundbreaking technologies.

Adaptive Learning: Building Customized Entrepreneurial Pathways

Predicting the future of entrepreneurship education invites us to consider an intensive, adaptive learning scenario. Current models in entrepreneurship education run the risk of restricting learning within the confines of fixed curriculum and generic solutions. However, AI and ML can be the game-changers, personalizing learning according to the learners' abilities, pace, and preferences.

An AI-powered entrepreneurship education curriculum might scan a learner's responses, analyze patterns, evaluate their comprehension and business acumen levels, and accordingly suggest bespoke learning paths. This way, the shifted focus from a one-size-fits-all model to adaptive learning can contribute significantly to the 'future-readiness' of our students.

Real-world Applications: Bridging the Gap

The future of entrepreneurship education lies in reducing the gap between classroom teachings and real-world applications. Entrepreneurship is rooted in applied learning – where theories intertwine with practice, fostering environments that encourage practical applications of learning will be pivotal. Simulated start-up environments, internship programs with successful entrepreneurs, or regular industrial visits may create a wholesome preparation ground for budding entrepreneurs.

Building A Global Perspective

Entrepreneurship today is not confined to geographical boundaries. Technology has not only made the world smaller but also opened a whole new realm of global opportunities. Therefore, the entrepreneurship curriculum of tomorrow must instill a sense of global perspective in students. Integration of international case studies, insights on global markets, and cultural nuances can provide students with a holistic understanding, preparing them to compete and collaborate at the global level.

Soft Skills: The Indispensable Element

While technical know-how and business acumen hold undeniable importance in entrepreneurship, the significance of soft skills cannot be downplayed. Emotional intelligence, leadership qualities, creativity, empathy, and resilience are the key differentiators in the entrepreneurial journey.

Fostering these skills from the classroom will shape robust, future-proof entrepreneurs. And hence, it is safe to foresee an educative future where soft skill development takes a more prominent role in the entrepreneurship curriculum.

=== Collaborative Efforts: The Power of Networking

The power of networks in the entrepreneurial world can't be stressed enough. In a digital age characterized by unprecedented connectedness, the capacity to form and leverage networks has been a defining factor in entrepreneurial success. Thus, fostering a network-oriented mindset, and providing students with opportunities to build, maintain, and navigate through professional networks will be a decisive element in the future of entrepreneurial education.

Circling back, the future of entrepreneurship education is hinged on the balance of various elements - technology, customization, practicality, global outlook, soft skills, and networking. Striking the right equilibrium won't be easy but necessary to prepare our students for an adventurous entrepreneurial journey. The stakes are high, but so are the rewards.